EXPLORING THE PAST

EXPLORING

CASTLES

Cliff Lines

Illustrated by Stephen Wheele

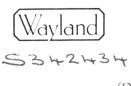

Exploring the Past

Editor: Elizabeth Summers
Designed by: David Armitage
Cover picture: Caernarfon Castle. One of the first castles to be built by King Edward I in Wales during the Middle Ages

First published in 1989 by
Wayland (Publishers) Ltd
61 Western Road, Hove
East Sussex, England BN3 1JD

British Library Cataloguing in Publication Data
Lines, C.J. (Clifford John), 1926–
    Exploring castles.–(Exploring the past)
    1. Great Britain. Castles
    I. Title II. Series
    941
ISBN 1 85210 456 2

Phototypeset by Kalligraphics Ltd, Horley, Surrey
Printed in Italy by G. Canale C.S.p.A., Turin
Bound in the UK by the Bath Press, Avon

Contents

1 Introduction

Have you ever explored a castle? There are nearly 200 castles in different parts of Britain and they are well worth a visit. Most are between six and nine hundred years old. In addition, there are places called castles, such as Cadbury Castle in Somerset, which were once hillforts. All the buildings have gone and only the earth banks and ditches can be seen.

The word 'castle' comes from the Roman words 'castellum' meaning a fortified camp and 'castrum' meaning fortified place. In this book we will look at castles and also at other forms of strongholds which were built for defence. In the pages which follow, there is advice on what to look for when you visit a castle and details of exciting models you can make. You will also find out how to plan and carry out a project on a stronghold near you.

Maiden Castle in Dorset is an Iron Age hillfort. The Romans captured the fort and the skeletons of the people killed in the fighting have been found nearby.

Are there any castles in your region? Name any two. Place names are useful guides to whether there has ever been a fortified camp or castle in an area. The words 'chester' (from 'castrum'), 'castle', 'caer' (Welsh for 'camp') and 'Dun' (Gaelic for 'fortified site') as part of a place name give a clue that there were once strongholds built there.

The central keep of Dover Castle was built in the 1180s and is surrounded by an inner and outer bailey.

2 | Hillforts

The first strongholds to be built in Britain were on hill tops and, in some cases, are nearly 3,000 years old. To make the hill top into a fort, deep ditches were dug round it and the earth thrown up as steep banks. Some, like Maiden Castle in Dorset, have three sets of banks. A wooden palisade (fence) or a stone wall was built along the highest bank with extra defences at the entrances. Many hillforts were built during the Iron Age (approximately 700BC–55BC).

Archaeologists are still finding out more about hillforts. The smallest, covering areas the size of two or three football pitches, were fortified farms or the huts of a few families. Some larger hillforts, like Danebury in Hampshire, were important settlements containing large numbers of huts arranged along streets. These were the homes of farmers and of craftsmen such as blacksmiths and weavers. Many hillforts in Scotland, such as the White and Brown Caterthuns of Angus, Tayside, were places intended for short-term refuge only. It is difficult today to imagine that these empty, wind-swept hill tops were once busy settlements. Those hillforts which were never lived in, like Walbury in Berkshire, were probably places where cattle were gathered for their protection.

In Scotland, in addition to hillforts, there are the remains of circular stone towers called brochs. Between the thick outer stone wall and the inner wall were small rooms and stairways. There were no windows on the outside of the broch and only one entrance. Smaller buildings nearby were protected by a stone wall around the

This hillfort at Beacon Hill in Hampshire has two sets of banks and extra protection at the entrance.

site. Small fortified enclosures, called duns, were also built throughout West Scotland during the Iron Age. Circular in shape, they had walls up to five metres thick and easily defended doorways.

Above Once the stronghold of a chief, Mousa Broch in the Shetlands was built with double walls which surround an inner courtyard.

what to look for at a hillfort

Cissbury, W. Sussex

Entrance

Bank

700 m

300 m

Entrance

Entrance

Make a rough plan of the shape, mark the entrances. Pace out the length and breadth, calculate distance in metres.

Draw a cross- section of the banks and ditches.

Ditch   Bank   Bank

Ditch

Caburn E. Sussex

Chalbury, Dorset

Bank

Ditch

Bank

Entrance

Bank

Draw a plan to show how the entrance was protected.

Curved Trench

Shallow Hole

Sketch any evidence that the site has been dug over by archaeologists.

Left This diagram shows the different features that can be found at a hillfort.

7

3 | Roman forts

After conquering Britain, the Romans stationed soldiers and support troops in forts which were specially built as military centres. The Roman army was highly organized and each fort was carefully planned with wide, straight streets meeting at right angles. The buildings were made of stone or timber and a stone wall surrounding the fort had watch towers and a protecting ditch. In the centre of the fort was a large headquarters building with the commanding officer's house nearby. The other officers had smaller houses while the troops lived in long barrack blocks. There were also workshops, storehouses, stables, a bath-house and a hospital. Outside the fort a settlement often grew up with shops, inns and an amphitheatre where troops were entertained.

A series of forts were built in Scotland with the most northerly at Inchtuthill near Dundee. They were built to repel attacks by the Picts (northern Britons). Others were built along

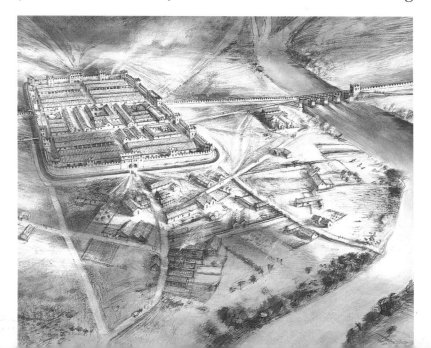

Chesters Roman Fort in Northumberland is one of the seventeen large forts built by the Romans along Hadrian's Wall. It was a cavalry fort defending the bridge across the North Tyne.

Hadrian's Wall and at places further south such as York and Caerleon in Wales. The foundations of these forts can still be seen and local museums contain relics which have been found in them. Roman forts were army bases, protected against sudden attack but not designed for a siege.

During the third century, southern England was threatened by foreign invaders once again, and the Romans built a row of forts along the coast. They include Pevensey and Porchester castles and were built for defence, unlike the garrison forts, which were designed as bases only.

In Scotland, the northern Britons continued to build hillforts, brochs and duns for defence. Dumbarton Castle (from 'Dun Breataun', meaning 'fortress of the Britons') was first built by the Celts as a fortified structure during the last years of the fifth century AD in Britain.

Above *Caerleon, a Roman legionary fortress in Gwent, was built with a large amphitheatre which could seat as many as 6,000 people.*

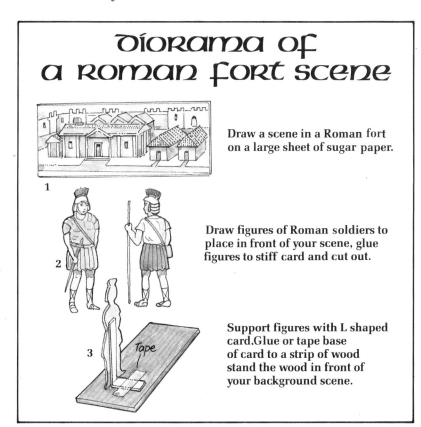

Diorama of a Roman fort scene

Draw a scene in a Roman fort on a large sheet of sugar paper.

Draw figures of Roman soldiers to place in front of your scene, glue figures to stiff card and cut out.

Support figures with L shaped card. Glue or tape base of card to a strip of wood stand the wood in front of your background scene.

Tape

Left *Follow the three easy steps to create your own diorama of a Roman fort scene.*

9

4 | Before the Norman invasion

Saxon strongholds

During the 600 years between Roman and Norman rule in Britain the country was invaded by groups of people from Europe. The first invaders were the Saxons who fought many battles with the British between AD 450 and 600. Later they had to defend themselves from Danish invaders. In the ninth century, King Alfred built a number of fortress towns, called 'burhs', to protect the west country from the Danes who had already settled in eastern England. These fortresses were oval or rectangular in shape and surrounded by a bank or ditch. Each fortress was kept in repair and garrisoned by local men with four men to defend each five metres of wall or earthwork.

Above *The King Alfred statue in Winchester. In Saxon times Winchester was the capital of Wessex. King Alfred fought off Danish invaders and built a network of fortified burhs throughout the region.*

Left *Burgh Castle in Suffolk is a Roman fort that was built to defend the coast against invasion by the Saxons.*

The Saxons also used the Roman walls standing round towns like York and Colchester. In towns such as Wallingford, Oxfordshire and Northampton some of the present streets were there in Saxon times. Unfortunately the wooden palisades and houses of the Saxon burhs have gone, but some earthworks can still be seen.

The solid stone church towers built by the Saxons were also probably used as strongholds which the villagers could shelter in when there was a raid. Earls Barton church in Northamptonshire has a large tower and is surrounded by earthworks which the Saxons may have built.

Sketch Saxon objects which are on display in a museum you can visit. In Scotland, look out for Pictish objects from this period. Picts were the ancient northern Britons who formed a vigorous kingdom in the north during the same period that the Saxons were settling in Britain.

5 Motte-and-bailey castles

When the Normans invaded England in 1066 they needed strongholds from which they could control the people they had conquered. There were no castles for them to capture so they quickly built their own. Each Norman lord was given a district to rule. In some instances, as in Scotland, the Normans were granted lands by the established rulers. The Scottish King David I and his successors actually invited the Normans to Scotland, where they built many castles.

A Norman lord would force the local people to build an earth mound by digging a wide, circular ditch and heaping the earth in the middle. Round the top of the mound, called a motte, a strong wooden palisade was put up. Inside the

This section of the Bayeux tapestry shows the building of the castle of Hastings shortly after the Norman invasion in 1066.

Above The circular motte of Castle Acre in Norfolk can be seen surrounded by a ditch. There are two baileys. The main one can be seen to the left of the motte.

palisade a wooden tower was built as a home and fortress for the lord and his soldiers. Below the motte a larger area, called the bailey, was levelled and then surrounded by a ditch and a palisade. Members of the lord's household lived in huts inside the bailey, which was also used for horses and cattle. The motte was reached across a bridge and by climbing wooden steps. These were removed during an attack. Sometimes more than one bailey was built and if there was water nearby the ditch round the motte-and-bailey was flooded.

After some years the wooden tower and palisades were replaced by stone or the site was no longer needed and was abandoned. Motte-and-bailey castles or their sites can be seen in many parts of the country. The Round Tower of Windsor Castle is built on a motte with a bailey on either side. At Pleshey in Essex only the site can be seen. Copy the drawing of a motte-and-bailey castle and label the following: motte, palisade, tower, bailey, household buildings. How easy would it be to attack or defend?

Right This illustration shows the general structure and position of the motte-and-bailey castle.

6 Keeps

The strongest building in a Norman castle was the keep. When William the Conqueror invaded in 1066 wooden keeps were hurriedly built on high ground. These were later replaced by square, stone towers like the White Tower of the Tower of London. Tower keeps had a basement and two or three other floors. The entrance was usually up a stairway on the outside wall. After 1100AD many more were built including those at Carlisle, Drum Castle, near Aberdeen, Rochester and Hedingham in Essex.

These square keeps had disadvantages. The corners collapsed if they were undermined (tunnelled beneath) and defenders had to lean out to shoot at attackers working at a corner. Towards the end of the twelfth century, rounded or many-sided keeps came into fashion. They had fewer blind spots and were stronger than square keeps. Keeps of this kind include Orford in Suffolk and Conisbrough in South Yorkshire.

Castles were also designed by building a circular stone wall around a small hill. This is called a curtain wall. Curtain walls have walkways near the top protected by battlements. Towers were built at points along the curtain wall to add strength. Rooms were built against the inside of the wall leaving a space in the middle. This type of castle is called a shell keep and examples include Cardiff, Windsor and Carisbrooke on the Isle of Wight.

If there is a keep at your nearest castle, make a sketch of it. Find out what type it is and if it has been altered since it was first built.

Above The Norman keep, Castle Rising, was built in Norfolk in about 1150. It is surrounded by a large bank and ditch which may be much older than the castle.

Below The wooden keep at Cardiff Castle was knocked down and rebuilt in stone in the twelfth century.

make a model of rochester castle

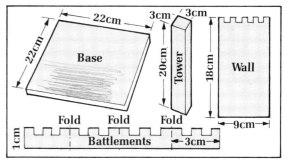

You will need:

Base of firm plywood or board, 22cm sq.
4 pieces of soft wood or balsa
   3cm sq. x 20cm high
4 strips of card 12cm long 1cm high shaped
   as battlements. Fold and glue to tops of
   towers.
4 pieces of card for walls shaped as shown.

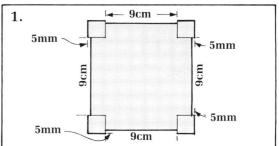

1.   Mark base board to position towers and
walls. Glue towers to base board. Use sticky
tape to glue walls to towers. 5mm in from
front of each tower glue walls to base.

2.   Cut card 15cm x 10cm and cut out
battlements. Fold as shown.

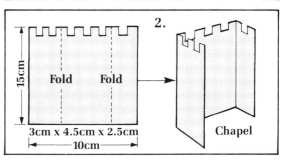

3.   Glue Chapel to model in position
shown.

4.   Make slope of balsa or card, place in
position as shown above.

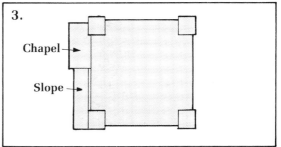

5.   Draw in windows and put doorway at
top of slope, see sketch below. Paint your
model.

Finished model of Rochester Castle.

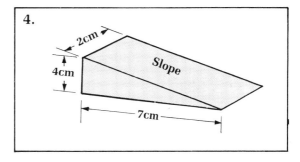

15

7 King Edward's Welsh castles

When Edward I became king in 1272, he found that there was a rebellion in Wales led by the Welsh Prince Llywelyn ap Gruffydd. Edward knew that, even after being defeated the Welsh followers of Prince Llywelyn would hide in the mountains of North Wales and attack his army when they least expected it. He therefore decided to build a ring of large castles around the coast which could be supplied by sea. The castles would be military centres, able to send troops to defeat any Welsh uprising.

The king put a skilled master mason, Master James of St. George, in charge of this building operation. Large numbers of workmen, stonemasons, quarrymen, carpenters and other craftsmen were drafted from all over England to build the castles. The first castles were built after Edward's first campaign in 1277 at Flint and Rhuddlan to command the route from Chester.

Above King Edward I reigned from 1272 to 1307, in which time he was responsible for the building of fourteen castles in Wales.

Below Caernarfon Castle was one of the first castles built by Edward I.

The most splendid castle was built at Caernarfon after the second campaign (1282–83). It was designed for the use of the king and his household when he was in Wales. In 1284, the king's wife, Eleanor, gave birth to their first son at Caernarfon. He was called Edward and was the first English Prince of Wales. The present Prince of Wales was given his title by the queen at a ceremony at Caernarfon in 1969.

In the thirty years after 1277 Edward I built fourteen castles in Wales, seven of which were in the north. By this time keeps had become unfashionable and stronger curtain walls with towers took their place. Concentric castles were also favoured. These were castles with two sets of walls, one enclosing the other. The inner wall was higher and much stronger than the outer enclosing wall, with a space between. Soldiers on the inner wall could fire over the heads of those on the outer wall and if attacking soldiers broke through the first wall they would be greeted by a hail of arrows, besides facing strong towers

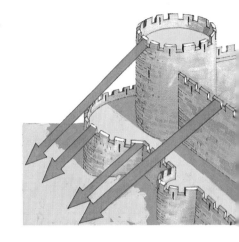

Above *This illustration shows the ways in which a castle with two walls would have been defended by archers.*

Below *The construction of Caerphilly Castle in mid-Glamorgan began in 1268. The moat was designed for maximum protection.*

and a gatehouse built into the second. Harlech and Beaumaris in North Wales were both concentric castles. Make a copy of the map below and use an atlas to name the seven castles – Beaumaris, Caernarfon, Conwy, Denbigh, Flint, Harlech and Rhuddlan. Now mark them on your map and give it a new title.

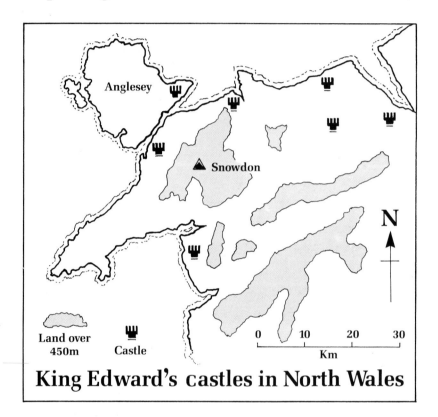

King Edward's castles in North Wales

This map shows the position of King Edward I's castles in North Wales.

Scottish castles

Having subdued his Welsh subjects for the time being, Edward's attention was soon drawn to rebellions in Scotland against English attempts to govern there. During the Wars of Independence (late thirteenth to early fourteenth centuries) Edward I and his son discovered that Scottish built castles such as Stirling, Edinburgh and Kildrummy could hold out against attack for long periods of time. The castle as a defensive structure was flourishing.

8 Defending a castle

Choosing a site

It was vital for castle builders of the Middle Ages to decide on the best site to build their castles. First it was important to know why the castle was being built. Some were needed to defend sea ports, some guarded routeways or river crossings, while some were a defence against invasion. When you visit a castle ask yourself, 'Why was a castle needed here?' The answer may be easy to spot. Ludlow Castle, for example was one of a chain built to guard the border between England and Wales (called the Marches). It also controlled river and road routeways. Sometimes conditions have changed since a castle was built making the answer more difficult to work out. When Pevensey Castle was built on the Sussex coast in 1067, the sea came close to its walls and the harbour was large enough for sailing ships. Today the castle is one-and-a-half kilometres from the sea and no ships can reach it.

Conwy Castle in Gwynedd, Wales was built between 1283 and 1287 and has eight towers. It overlooks the town of Conwy which is surrounded by a wall built at the same time as the castle.

Above *Stirling Castle, built on a rock overlooking the Forth Valley in Scotland, was an important stronghold for the Scottish Kings.*

The second question to ask about a castle is, 'Why was the site chosen?' Many were built on high ground, especially constructed mounds, or the edge of a cliff where attack was difficult and lookouts in the castle could see the enemy approaching from a long way off. Castles were seldom built on a river bank for fear of flooding. Instead the site chosen was on higher ground where a stream might be dammed to make a moat. Caerlaverock Castle in Dumfries, southern Scotland, was protected by a moat in this way. Stirling Castle in Scotland was built on a rock, in an ideal place for surveying the surrounding countryside for many kilometres.

Copy the map below and mark on it two castles: one to defend the port from attack from the sea; the other to control the routeways through the hills thus defending the castle from land attack. List the reasons for the sites you have chosen.

Right *Where would you site your castle on this map?*

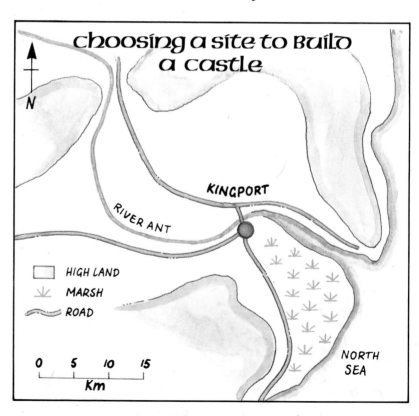

choosing a site to Build a castle

N

KINGPORT

RIVER ANT

HIGH LAND

MARSH

ROAD

0   5   10   15
Km

NORTH SEA

Protecting the entrances

The entrance to the castle was always the weakest spot and had to be given special protection. Some, like Conwy in North Wales had a defensive wall with turrets, called a barbican, to shield the gateway. If there was a moat or ditch, a drawbridge was used to make the approach difficult. The entrance door was usually part of a massive gatehouse complete with towers and arrow slits. Very often a portcullis protected the entrance. It was a grille made of wood and iron which was lowered down grooves in the gateway. Look for these grooves when you visit a castle; the portcullis may no longer be there. Some gatehouses had two or three sets of portcullises; Caernarfon had six! Attackers

Attack on castles were often furious and bloody. Many soldiers died from Greek fire, arrow wounds or drowning.

Moat

Hoards

Portcullis

Greek Fire

could find themselves trapped between them in a 'killing ground'. At Bodiam Castle in East Sussex there were three portcullises with an inner door leading into the courtyard. the door would be barred from inside the gatehouse so that attackers who had reached the courtyard over the walls could not open the main gate to let friends in.

There might also be a parapet overhanging the gateway with machicolations (openings in the floor). Defenders could drop things through these openings on to the enemy below. Pouring a substance called 'Greek fire' was very effective. Arrows could be fired from the gatehouse towers and 'murder holes' in the roof could also be used by the defenders.

When you visit a castle, study the entrance carefully to see how it was defended. The chart below is a check list of the things to look for. Make a copy of the chart without the sketches, leaving spaces for your own drawings of the entrance to a castle you visit.

Above *Alnwick Castle in Northumberland was built to defend the border against the Scots and has been the home of the Percy family since 1309.*

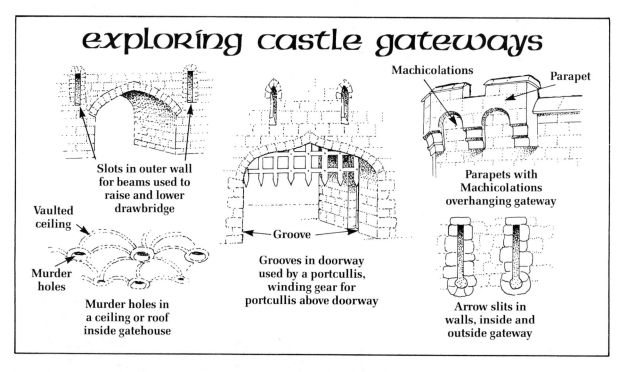

exploring castle gateways

Slots in outer wall for beams used to raise and lower drawbridge

Vaulted ceiling

Murder holes

Murder holes in a ceiling or roof inside gatehouse

Groove

Grooves in doorway used by a portcullis, winding gear for portcullis above doorway

Machicolations

Parapet

Parapets with Machicolations overhanging gateway

Arrow slits in walls, inside and outside gateway

Living through a siege

Before the days of gunpowder, castles were attacked with a variety of devices. Rocks were hurled by huge machines; doors were broken down by using battering rams; scaling ladders and wooden siege towers (called belfries) were used to scale the walls.

What the defenders feared most, however, was being undermined by tunnellers digging under the building. When Rochester Castle was besieged in 1215 by King John a tunnel was dug under part of the castle and supported by wooden props while the men were tunnelling. The fat of forty pigs was used, together with the props and straw to make a fire in the tunnel which caused a corner of the building to collapse, leaving an opening for the attackers. The repair to the damage can still be seen.

Below left Raglan Castle in Gwent was built in the fifteenth century. The castle was badly damaged during the Civil War siege of 1646.

Below right The illustration shows how the enemy would go about undermining a castle.

Undermining a castle

Castles had to be able to stand up to a siege. Sufficient stores of food and weapons had to be kept and the garrison had to be large enough to resist attack but not so large that it put a strain on provisions. A well giving fresh water was needed and many castles also had a dovecot to provide supplies of fresh meat. When Kenilworth Castle was besieged by Henry III in 1266 the garrison was able to hold out for six months until they became short of food and other supplies.

When you visit a castle find out the ways it was protected from different kinds of attack. For example, a moat made tunnelling very difficult and prevented a siege tower being used. Notice how thick the walls are. Look for ways in which the castle could stand up to a siege. Many have underground store rooms, wells and methods of collecting rain water.

Entering a castle was always the enemy's worst difficulty in overthrowing its owner. A siege tower, trebuchet or battering ram were three ways to overcome this.

9 | The castle as a home

Have you ever wondered what it was like to live in a medieval castle? It was a home for the lord and his family, his servants, workmen and soldiers. The most important room was the great hall. All the members of the lord's household ate their meals in the hall at trestle tables. The lord's family and guests sat at one end on a raised platform. Looking at ruined castles today, it is sometimes hard to imagine what they were like. The timber floors of the great halls have rotted away, but the stone supports or slots can often be seen in the walls. A fireplace and large windows are also clues to help you to identify the hall.

Food was cooked in a kitchen nearby. This is easy to find, because it will have at least one large fireplace and usually a well for water. The food was served from a small room called the pantry while ale and wine were served from the buttery.

This cutaway illustration shows the layout of a Norman keep.

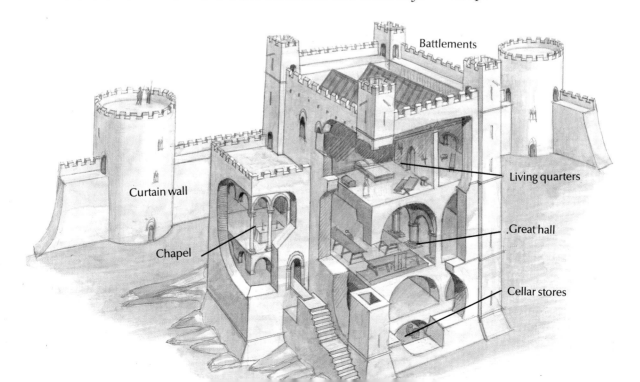

Battlements

Curtain wall

Chapel

Living quarters

Great hall

Cellar stores

These two rooms are usually between the kitchen and the hall. Small rooms on the floor above the hall or leading from it were sleeping chambers for the family and were called the solar. Members of the household slept on benches or straw in the hall itself. Lavatories, called garderobes, were rooms about one metre square and set into the outside walls. Look for the shaft which took the sewage down into a pit or the moat.

If you find a room with a more elaborate window, a small stone basin and a seat set into the wall, it is likely to be the chapel.

Make sketches like those below of clues you find in a castle about the rooms in which people lived. Do not forget that castles also served as prisons. Look for small basement rooms that may have been dungeons. Find out if the castle has ever held any famous prisoners.

The features typical in a castle vary from place to place as this illustration shows.

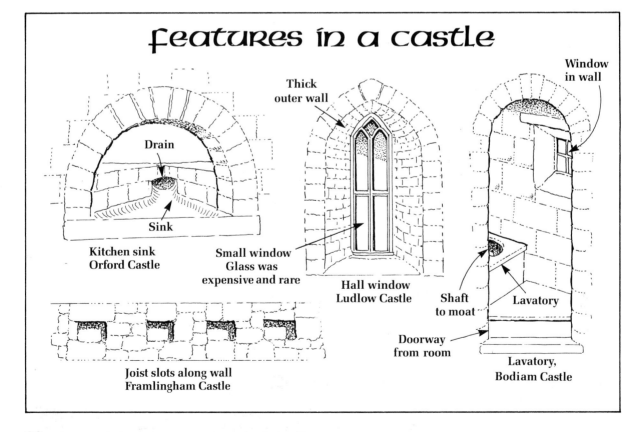

features in a castle

Drain

Sink

**Kitchen sink
Orford Castle**

**Joist slots along wall
Framlingham Castle**

Thick
outer wall

**Small window
Glass was
expensive and rare**

**Hall window
Ludlow Castle**

Window
in wall

Shaft
to moat

Lavatory

Doorway
from room

**Lavatory,
Bodiam Castle**

10 Medieval times

Moated manors and fortified homes

While the powerful nobles of medieval Britain lived in castles, wealthy merchants and farmers lived in manor houses with towers and battlements and often surrounded by a moat. The defences were not very strong and would not have protected the people inside if the manor had been attacked. The moats were not usually very wide. They were a difficult barrier to cross for thieves or bands of outlaws but would only have slowed down a powerful attack. The people who lived in moated manor houses were not trying to protect themselves from attack. They wanted to show their friends and others that they were important people and could afford a building which was almost as grand as a castle.

The sixteenth-century gatehouse of Stokesay Castle in Shropshire. A fortified manor house, it was originally built in the twelfth and thirteenth centuries.

The moat was often used as a fishpond in which carp were kept and it was also a store of water which could be used if there was a fire. These moated manor houses can be seen in many country districts and some are open to the public. Some moats have been drained or turned into garden ponds. One of the finest fortified manors is Stokesay Castle in Shropshire. It was built by a very rich wool merchant in the thirteeth century and is surrounded by a moat.

Some moated manor houses are said to be haunted by people who lived there in medieval or later times. Find out if there are any ghost stories connected with castles or manors in your area. Write a story about a haunted manor. You could make it into a play, which you and some friends could record on tape and play to the class. Remember to include suitably spine-chilling sound effects!

The great hall of a fortified manor house as it may have looked seven hundred years ago.

A knight's castle home

Bodiam Castle in East Sussex was built at the end of the fourteenth century by Sir Edward Dalyngrigge as a protection against French raiders. The castle was designed as a comfortable home for the knight and his family, and also as a fortress. Bodiam is a rectangular castle with towers and a large central courtyard. It is surrounded by a moat which could at one time be crossed at two points. Although many of the rooms are in ruins the castle contains many clues as to how an important medieval lord and his family lived.

At ground level there were two halls where food was served, one for the lord and his guests and the other for the servants. Near these halls were kitchens, a pantry, a well and a pigeon loft or dovecot to provide fresh meat. There was a

The main gatehouse of Bodiam Castle in East Sussex is positioned in the centre of the structure, protected by a moat and two massive towers. The oak portcullis, plated with iron, is still in place above the entrance.

large chamber where the lord could receive guests and a smaller room for family use. The lord also had a chapel with a small room for the priest.

On the other side of the courtyard were the rooms of the garrison. On the first floor there were bedrooms and lavatories with many smaller rooms in the towers. Fireplaces warmed these rooms in winter and windows let in light from the courtyard. Bodiam was never attacked and was a home for important families until the seventeenth century when much of the interior was destroyed.

Make a copy of the plan below and use different colours to show the lord's rooms, the servants' and those of the garrison.

This plan of the ground floor of Bodiam Castle shows the layout of the rooms, towers, courtyard and entrances.

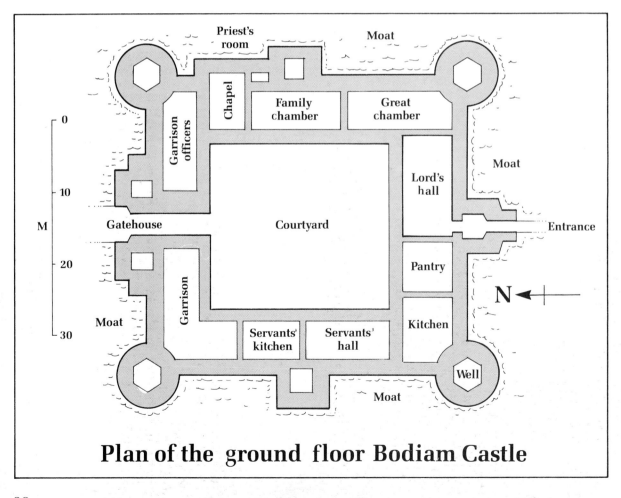

Plan of the ground floor Bodiam Castle

11 | Tower houses

Gradually, the need for castles began to lessen in most parts of England and Wales in the fourteenth century. In Scotland, Ireland and northern England, however, important landowners built fortified homes called tower houses. They had strong, stone walls and could be defended like a castle although they were not as large or as expensive to build. Tower houses protected the owner and his family from raids by sheep or cattle stealers, during quarrels between neighbouring families, and from border warfare between England and Scotland. The tower house, called a pele tower in Scotland and northern England, was usually rectangular with small windows. Designs did vary, however. Behind the main door there was often a second door made of iron in the shape of a grille. There was always a guardroom nearby and a narrow staircase leading to the rooms above and other floors.

Built in 1628, Braemar Castle in Grampian, Scotland has a central tower and an underground dungeon.

Pele tower in Cocklaw, Northumberland, was a tower house built in the fifteenth century to protect the border with Scotland.

The ground floor was used as a store and included a loft above a wooden ceiling. The family lived on the first floor where there was a hall, a kitchen and other smaller rooms. The servants slept in a loft over the hall. Sometimes a courtyard protected by a stone wall, called a barmkin in Scotland, surrounded the tower house. It was used to shelter animals.

The first tower houses were built in the fourteenth century and they continued to be built for three hundred years. By the sixteenth century their design had become more elaborate and often included gun-ports and steeply sloping roofs.

Explain why each of the following features of a tower house helped protect it if it was suddenly attacked: small windows; a second inner door; narrow winding stairways; living rooms on the first floor.

Castles lose their importance

By 1506, when Henry VIII came to the throne, the days of castle building were almost over. Castles were no longer necessary and were frowned upon by the king. Modern weapons had become more than a match for castle walls by this time. During the fifteenth century, cannons had become safer to use and were less likely to blow up the gunners who fired them. They were also more accurate and had sufficient power to make a hole in a solid stone wall. England and Wales were also more peaceful places with the power of the wealthy lords taken away by the king. Royal approval had to be obtained to build a castle. The Duke of Buckingham was beheaded for building a castle in Gloucestershire without Henry VIII's permission. The king did not want

A page from The Art of Gunnery *(1608) by Thomas Smith illustrates a castle under attack. Both attackers and defenders are using cannons.*

King Henry VIII, king of England from 1509 to 1547.

any of his lords to become too powerful and threaten his rule.

Castles were no longer needed when the country was at peace. Many were made more comfortable by adding windows to let in more light and by building doors to make them more convenient places to live in. Some lords abandoned their castles to live in large houses which were given turrets and battlements but were not designed as fortresses.

Find pictures of weapons used in the sixteenth and seventeenth centuries. Draw a sketch of a castle being attacked by artillery.

12 Henry VIII's coastal forts

In 1538, during the reign of King Henry VIII there was great panic when the kings of France and Spain threatened to invade England. King Henry quickly built a number of castles along the coast as a precaution. Although they are called castles, no lords lived in them and they were really military forts where soldiers could be stationed and guns could be positioned. The forts protected the entrance to the River Thames and harbours along the south coast, including Portsmouth and Falmouth. They were designed with many gun-ports pointing in all directions.

Like some medieval castles, there was a central keep where the garrison lived, with store rooms nearby for guns and ammunition. Some forts were surrounded by a dry moat and the entrance could only be reached along a wooden bridge and across a drawbridge. These forts were the first designed for use by artillery and to withstand attack by cannon balls. The buildings were kept low and rounded and built in layers so that guns could be fired from different levels.

Built around 1540 by Henry VIII, Deal Castle was part of the defences prepared against a possible invasion by the French. It has 145 gun openings and is protected by a moat.

Behold your King

THE ILE OF WAIT

Right *King Charles I was held prisoner at Carisbrooke Castle on the Isle of Wight from November 1647 to December 1648. This sketch was made a few months before the king was executed in London.*

The invasion never took place and some of the coastal forts have disappeared. Several are museums, including the largest and most complete at Deal in Kent. Make a sketch of the photograph of Deal Castle on page 35 and add the following captions: dry moat; keep; gun-ports; drawbridge; parapet.

During the rule of Oliver Cromwell (1653–1658) castles owned by people who had supported the king, Charles I, in the Civil War, were destroyed or damaged. Local people were allowed to take away stones to build with and only ruins remain, like those of Corfe Castle which is in Dorset.

Right *Corfe Castle in Dorset was destroyed during the Civil War and only the ruins remain.*

13 | The last three centuries

Fortresses in Scotland 1688–1800

Fortresses played an important part in Scotland's history between 1688 and 1800. When King James II was forced to leave the throne in 1688, he and his descendants found many loyal supporters (known as Jacobites) in Scotland. Government forces built forts throughout the Highlands to impose law and order on these supporters. At this time Fort William, Fort Augustus and the Garrison at Inversnaid (Loch Lomond) were built.

Defence against Napoleon

Strongholds have always been built near the coast when an invasion has been feared. During the war with France at the beginning of the

Above An old print of Fort William in Scotland. The fort was built in 1655 as a defence against the Highlanders. It was pulled down two hundred years later.

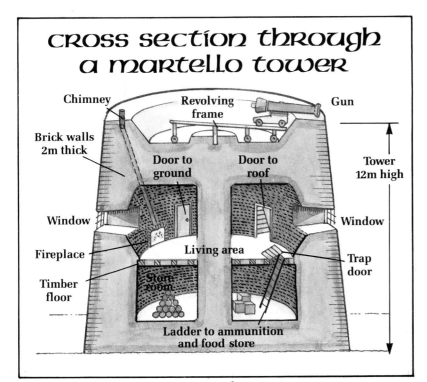

CROSS SECTION THROUGH A MARTELLO TOWER

Chimney
Revolving frame
Gun
Brick walls 2m thick
Door to ground
Door to roof
Tower 12m high
Window
Window
Fireplace
Living area
Trap door
Timber floor
Store room
Ladder to ammunition and food store

Left A Martello tower, showing the thickness of the walls, the flat roof to take cannons and the inside layout.

nineteenth century, the French leader Napoleon Bonaparte, threatened to invade Britain. As a result work was started in 1805 on a series of gun towers along the east and south coasts of England. They were called Martello towers and were round with a flat roof on which a cannon could be placed. About half a million bricks were needed to build each tower and the walls were extremely thick. Inside there was a store room for food, water and ammunition. On the floor above there were three rooms grouped around the central pillar. These were for the officer and the twenty-four soldiers who made up the garrison.

The entrance door to the tower was placed about six metres above the ground and could only be reached by a ladder or drawbridge. The towers differed slightly in their design and some were surrounded by a moat like a medieval castle. Martello towers were also built in Ireland, Jersey and Orkney. Britain was never invaded and, after the

Above *Napoleon Bonaparte in 1809. His threats to invade England led to the building of the Martello towers along the south and east coasts.*

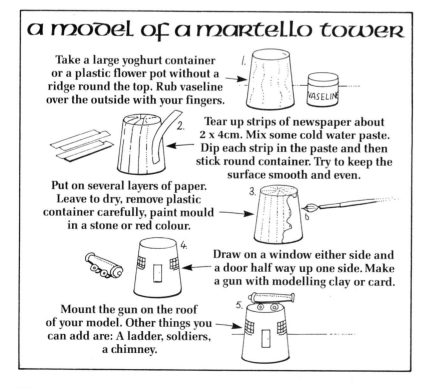

a model of a martello tower

1. Take a large yoghurt container or a plastic flower pot without a ridge round the top. Rub vaseline over the outside with your fingers.

2. Tear up strips of newspaper about 2 x 4cm. Mix some cold water paste. Dip each strip in the paste and then stick round container. Try to keep the surface smooth and even.

3. Put on several layers of paper. Leave to dry, remove plastic container carefully, paint mould in a stone or red colour.

4. Draw on a window either side and a door half way up one side. Make a gun with modelling clay or card.

5. Mount the gun on the roof of your model. Other things you can add are: A ladder, soldiers, a chimney.

Left *This illustration shows how to make your own model of a Martello tower.*

defeat of Napoleon in 1815, some of the towers became coastguard look-outs. Over the years some have been washed away by the sea, some have become private homes, while some have been turned into museums.

In addition to Martello towers, three larger fortresses, called Redoubts, were built at Harwich, Dymchurch and Eastbourne.

Strongholds built in recent times

In medieval times castles were built by rich and powerful men, and down the ages their sturdy towers and parapets have become a symbol of power and security.

In Victorian times it was fashionable to have buildings designed with battlements like castles. You may see water towers or the entrances to railway tunnels disguised in this way. Balmoral Castle, the queen's home on Royal Deeside, Scotland, looks like a medieval castle, but it was not built until 1849. Castell Coch, near Cardiff in Wales, is another Victorian fairy-tale castle.

Above Castell Coch in South Glamorgan, Wales, is just over one hundred years old and was built like a fairy-tale castle by the Marquess of Bute.

Left The Victorian estate buildings in Bradford were built with towers and turrets like a castle. This was a popular fashion with architects at the time, influenced by the great castles of Britain.

The last large private house to be designed like a castle was built about sixty years ago in Devon. It is called Castle Drogo and is built of large blocks of granite on the edge of a steep cliff.

Defence agains invasion 1939–45

The most recent threat of invasion to Britain came from Germany during the Second World War (1939–45), and strong concrete pillboxes were built from which soldiers could fire at the enemy. Many of these pillboxes can still be seen. Those along the coast are often wholly or partially covered by sand. Why do you think this is? You can also still see the rows of concrete blocks and steep ditches, called tank traps, set up to stop advancing tanks.

Make sketches of real and fake strongholds in your area, using the chart below. Perhaps a class excursion could be arranged to local sites.

Real and fake strongholds of the 19th and 20th centuries

Second World War pillbox guarding a road

Second World War anti-tank concrete blocks.

Fake turrets with parapets with gaps at regular intervals (crenellated) used to disguise water tower or railway tunnel

Fake towers of large house built in 19th Century

Long narrow windows in the walls of a house which is not very old

Strongholds have changed over the centuries, but many still imitate those of the past.

14 | A castle project

Now is the time for you to explore strongholds in your district. You may like to explore them with some friends. For safety, you may also need to take an adult with you. You may be lucky enough to have a medieval castle near you, but, if not, there are plenty of other fortifications to explore, such as Martello towers, Roman forts and hillforts.

A good detective always prepares well in advance and uses the proper equipment to carry out investigations. Here is a plan of action.

● Decide with friends which stronghold would be the best to explore in your district. Not all castles can be visited and some hillforts are difficult to reach.

● Decide how you are going to use the information you find out when you explore the stronghold. You may like to: write a project book about the stronghold; make a castle trail which will help people to see the most interesting parts of the castle; make a guide book which other children of your age would find more interesting than existing guides.

Harlech Castle in Gwynedd was one of Edward I's Welsh castles. The rectangular castle is protected by two sets of walls.

● Plan a quiz containing questions which you are likely to want answered when you visit the site. Leave space for the answers and for other questions which occur to you during the visit. Leave room for sketches. Below is the first page of a quiz prepared by children who visited a Martello tower.

Equipment you will find useful

You will need a clipboard and some sheets of paper for notes and sketches; a pencil and rubber and, if possible, a camera. Finally, a measuring tape is useful for finding out such things as the thickness of the walls and the height and the depth of the arrow slits.

Researching your project

After your visit you will need to use your local reference library to find out more about the strong-hold and its history. Photocopy any drawings you may need.

A castle guide

To write a castle guide for young people you will need to plan your chapters or sections, starting

This example of a quiz will help you to make up your own when you visit a castle. This quiz is from a visit to a Martello tower.

Visit to a Martello Tower

Name *James Allaway*   Date *5th February*

1 What material was used to build the walls? *Bricks*
2 How many floors are there ? *2*
3 How many rooms are there in the living quarters? *3 (1 for the officer, 2 for the Soldiers)*
4 What is the name of the room where the gunpowder was kept ? *Magazine*
5 How did the soldiers get to the lower floor? *Through a trap door and down a ladder*
6 Where was the gun ? *On the roof*
7 How did they store water? *In the tank under the floor*
8 How many officers and men lived in the tower? *1 officer and 24 men*
9 When was the tower built ? *About 1804*
10 What was there around the tower ? *A Moat*

---

with an introduction to the castle and its history. Sections will also be needed on the main places to be visited, such as the gatehouse, kitchens and great hall. Write your guide so that it helps the visitor to find his or her way round and add illustrations. A final section on the castle, who owns it and when it is open to the public will help to make the guide a useful souvenir.

A page from a guide to Pevensey Castle, made by schoolchildren who visited the castle. It combines directions, illustrations, information and history.

Pevensey Castle

Cross the moat by the wooden bridge to the gatehouse. This was built about 1200 A.D. Not much is left of the two towers.

In each of the towers there is a dungeon. The tower on the right has a stairway which leads down to the dungeon. Inside the dungeon there are no windows. It is shaped like this.

The roof is shaped like the inside of a barrel. Imagine what it was like to be a prisoner in this cold dark place!

In the other tower the dungeon is worse. The only way in is through a trap in the roof. There are no windows and the walls are covered in slime. It is called oubliette from the French word 'to forget'. Prisoners put down there could be forgotten about. No one knows if any came out alive!

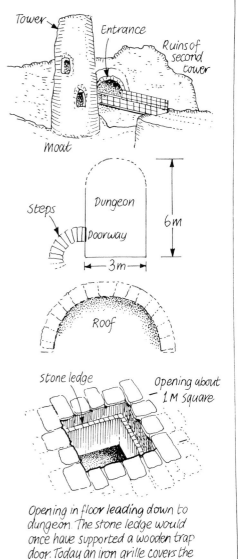

Opening in floor leading down to dungeon. The stone ledge would once have supported a wooden trap door. Today an iron grille covers the opening to stop people falling in.

strongholds time chart

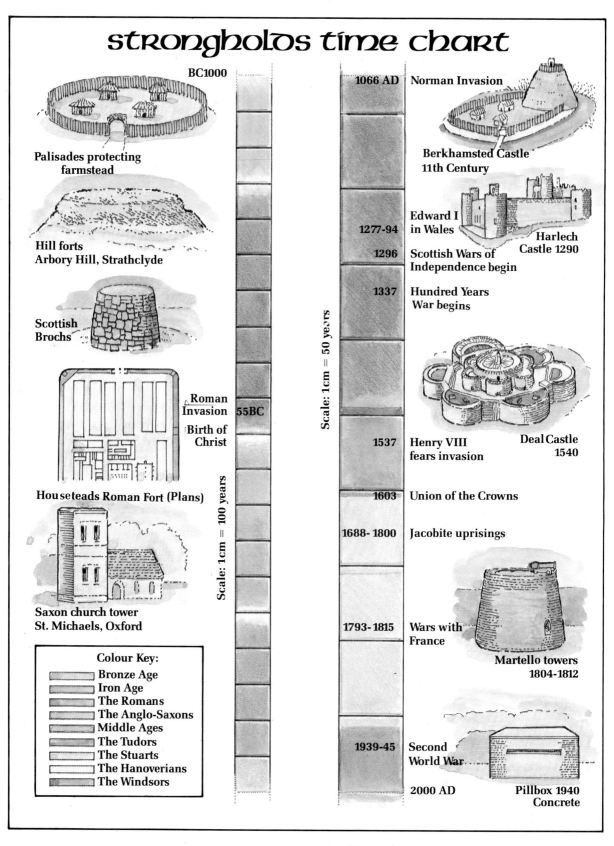

BC1000

Palisades protecting
farmstead

Hill forts
Arbory Hill, Strathclyde

Scottish
Brochs

Roman
Invasion   55BC

Birth of
Christ

Houseteads Roman Fort (Plans)

Saxon church tower
St. Michaels, Oxford

Scale: 1cm = 100 years

Colour Key:
- Bronze Age
- Iron Age
- The Romans
- The Anglo-Saxons
- Middle Ages
- The Tudors
- The Stuarts
- The Hanoverians
- The Windsors

Scale: 1cm = 50 years

1066 AD	Norman Invasion
	Berkhamsted Castle 11th Century
1277-94	Edward I in Wales
	Harlech Castle 1290
1296	Scottish Wars of Independence begin
1337	Hundred Years War begins
1537	Henry VIII fears invasion
	Deal Castle 1540
1603	Union of the Crowns
1688-1800	Jacobite uprisings
1793-1815	Wars with France
	Martello towers 1804-1812
1939-45	Second World War
2000 AD	Pillbox 1940 Concrete

Places to visit

Strongholds can be found in all parts of Britain and most can be visited. Remember that some buildings will have been altered in recent times with pieces added which look old but are not. For example, the Round Tower at Windsor and other parts of the castle were altered in the nineteenth century. Add other places you visit to this list.

Broch: Dun Telve, Highlands,; Moussa, Shetland.
Castles – Built by Edward I: Caernarfon, Gwynedd; Conwy, Gwynedd.
    – Motte-and-bailey: Berkhamsted, Hertfordshire; Windsor, Berkshire.
    – Norman keeps: Carrickfergus, Antrim; Colchester, Essex; Orford, Suffolk;
Tower of London.
    – On an island: Kissimul, Barra.
    – Other: Bodiam, East Sussex (built 1385 with moat); Edinburgh, Lothian;
Hever, Kent (built in thirteenth century):; Stirling, Central (built
in the fifteenth century as a Royal castle).
Fake strongholds: Balmoral, Aberdeenshire; Castell Coch, near Cardiff.
Hillforts: Caburn, East Sussex; Danebury, Hampshire; Figsbury, Wiltshire;
    Maiden Castle, Dorset; Moel-y-Gaer, Flint; The Caterthuns, Angus.
Moated Manors: Ightam Mote, Kent (fourteenth century); Oxburgh Hall, Norfolk (fifteenth century);
    Stokesay Castle, Shrophire (thirteenth century).
Martello towers: Clacton-on-Sea, Essex; Dymchurch, Kent; Eastbourne, East Sussex.
Roman forts: Chesters, Northumberland; Corbridge, Northumberland; Hardknott, Cumbria;
    Housesteads, Northumberland; Inchtuthill, Tayside; Porchester Castle,
    Hampshire; Richborough Castle, Kent.
Tower houses: Clara, Kilkenny (fifteenth century); Claypotts, Tayside (sixteenth
    century); Craigievar Castle, Grampian (seventeenth century); Hermitage, Borders.
Tudor forts: Deal, Kent; St Mawes, Cornwall.

Further reading

Baker, S., *Castles* (Macdonald Educational, 1976)

Branigan, K., *Roman Britain* (Readers Digest, 1980)

Breeze, D.J., *Roman Forts in Britain* (Shire, 1983)

Clark, R., *Castles* (Wayland, 1985)

Davison, B., *Explore a castle* (Hamish Hamilton, 1982)

James, Alan, *Castles and Mansions* (Wayland, 1988)

Sanchez, S., *The Castle Story* (Penguin, 1979)

Sorrell, A., *British Castles* (Batsford, 1973)

Vaughan, Jenny, *Castles* (Franklin Watts, 1984)

Woodlander, D., and Brown, J., *Castles* (A C Black, 1986)

Videos
Castle Clues, produced by the Royal Armouries at the Tower of London, London EC3N 4AB

Glossary

Amphitheatre A building used for exhibitions, games and other events in which the seats are placed above one another around an open space.

Archaeologists People who study ruins and other evidence to find out what life was like in the past.

Artillery Large guns used in fighting on land.

Bailey The outer defences of a Norman castle, usually protected by a wall and moat.

Barbican A wall or tower which protected a gateway from a direct attack.

Barmkin A small courtyard protected by a wall attached to a tower house.

Battlements A wall or parapet which is crenellated.

Brochs Fortified circular towers built for defence in Scotland.

Burhs Fortified Saxon towns usually protected by a wall of timber or stone.

Concentric castles Castles which were built with two sets of walls, one enclosed inside the other.

Crenellated The name given to a parapet which has gaps at regular intervals.

Duns Small, fortified enclosures built throughout West Scotland from the Iron Age to the early Saxon period.

Fortified Built to protect from attack. The word comes from the Latin meaning 'to make strong'.

Garrison The soldiers living in a fortress to defend it.

Gun-ports Openings in a wall with round holes to take a muzzle of a gun, and slits to see through.

Hadrian's Wall Great wall built on the orders of the Roman Emperor Hadrian in 122AD. It acted as a northern frontier between the Rivers Tyne and Solway, used for defence against the 'barbarians' of the north.

Hillfort A hill top which was protected from attack by surrounding mounds and ditches.

Iron Age The period from about the seventh century BC until the coming of the Romans in 55BC.

Jacobites Supporters of James II when he was deposed from the English throne in 1688.

Machicolations The openings in the floor of an overhanging parapet used to drop things on the enemy.

Martello towers Round or oval towers built during the war with France at the beginning of the nineteenth century to protect the east and south coasts.

Medieval times The period from approximately 1066 until 1500AD.

Moat A ditch or wide channel usually filled with water to protect a castle or manor.

Motte The mount or hill on which a Norman castle was built. The motte was often surrounded by a water-filled moat or ditch.

Murder holes Openings in the roof of a gatehouse which were used to drop things on to attackers below.

Oubliette A prison cell where prisoners could be left and forgotten about.

Palisade A wooden wall or fence built for protection.

Parapet A stone wall which screens the walkway used by soldiers on the roof of a tower or castle.

Pillboxes Concrete shelters with gun slots used to defend a routeway or a building.

Portcullis A wood and metal gate which slides up and down in grooves.

Redoubts Large fortified strongholds built during the war with France at the beginning of the nineteenth century. They could house 350 troops and acted as a support to the Martello tower defences.

Shell keep A keep built in the form of a high circular wall. Buildings were built against the inside of the wall and towers spaced along the wall gave extra protection.

Tower house Large stone buildings like a keep found in northern England, Scotland and Ireland. They were fortified homes which could be defended.

Trebuchet A large catapult used for hurling rocks and stones at the enemy.

Picture acknowledgements
The publishers would like to thank the following for providing the photographs in this book: Aldus Archive 6, 7 (top); The Mansell Collection 11 (bottom); Mary Evans Picture Library 11 (top), 37 (top); Michael Holford 12; Ronald Sheridan's Ancient Art & Architecture Collection 5, 20 (top), 32; Topham Picture Library 22 (top), 27, 29, 31, 33, 35, 36 (bottom); Wales Tourist Board 9, (top), 14 (bottom), 16 (bottom), 17 (bottom), 23 (left), 39 (top), 41; Wayland Picture Library 4, 8, 10 (both), 13 (top), 14 (top), 16 (top), 19, 34, 36 (top), 38 (top).
The illustrations on pages 7, 9, 15, 18, 20, 22, 23, 26, 30, 37, 38, 40, 42, 43 & 44 were provided by Steve Wheele. All additional artwork by John James.

Index